Our Discovery Island

3

STUDENT BOOK

Space Island

Aaron Jolly • José Luis Morales
Series Advisor: David Nunan

Series Consultants:
Hilda Martínez • Xóchitl Arvizu

Advisory Board:
Tim Budden • Tina Chen • Betty Deng • Dr. Nam-Joon Kang
Dr. Wonkey Lee • Wenxin Liang • Ann Mayeda • Wade O. Nichols • Jamie Zhang

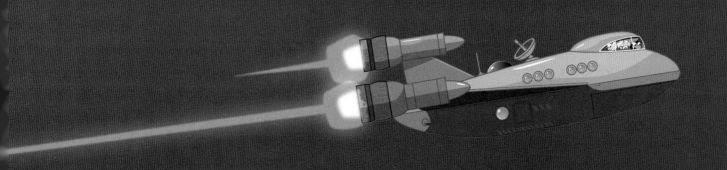

Pearson Education Limited
Edinburgh Gate
Harlow
Essex CM20 2JE
England
and Associated Companies throughout the world.

Our Discovery Island ™

www.ourdiscoveryisland.com

© Pearson Education Limited 2012

Based on the work of Sagrario Salaberri

Phonics syllabus and activities by Rachel Wilson

First published 2012
Seventeenth impression 2020

ISBN: 978-1-4479-0063-4

Set in Longman English 14/18pt

Printed in China (GCC/17)

Illustrators: Humberto Blanco (Sylvie Poggio Artists Agency), Anja Boretzki (Good Illustration), Scott Burroughs (Deborah Wolfe), Chan Cho Fai, Lee Cosgrove, Leo Cultura, Marek Jagucki, Mark Ruffle (The Organisation), and Dickie Seto

Picture Credits: The Publishers would like to thank the following for their kind permission to reproduce their photographs: (Key: b-bottom; c-center; l-left; r-right; t-top) Alamy Images: Arco Images GmbH 46br, Blend Images 94tl, Bon Appetit 95br, dbimages 94br, Danita Delimont 22bl, EuroCreon Co.Ltd 23r, Glowimages RM 71l, Sally and Richard Greenhill 70r, Juniors Bildarchiv 47cr, Dennis MacDonald 22tr, Simon Reddy 95tr, Visual&Written SL 39l, Simon Whaley 54l; Trevor Clifford: 25, 37, 49, 54 (tiles / stones), 58b, 63l, 63r, 73, 78, 97; Corbis: Beau Lark 66 (4), Nik Wheeler 74 (f); Tina Gao: 71r; Getty Images: Altrendo Travel 75r, Iconica / Jamie Grill 66 (2); iStockphoto: gabrieldome 94tr, Eric Isselée 47 (duck), Kyu Oh 23l, Hannu Liivaar 47 (parrot), mandygodbehear 66 (5), Ekaterina Monakhova 70l, Alexey Tkachenko 75l, Csaba Vanyi 58tc; OceanwideImages. com: Gary Bell 30tc; Photolibrary.com: Foodpix 66 (1), Fresh Food Images 95c, Imagestate RM 94bl, Pacific Stock / Sri Maiava Rusden 46tr, White / Ryan McVay 66 (3); Rex Features: 87, J. Barry Peake 30bl; Shutterstock.com: 2happy 14 (c), 39r, 74 (g), Akva 98 (c), Potapov Alexander 14 (a), 21b (5a), Ambient Ideas 14 (d), Andresr 33 (4b), Subbotina Anna 33 (1a), 45 (6b), Yuri Arcurs 13r, 33 (3a), 105 (2a), 105 (3b), Asbe 47 (iguana), Avava 98 (e), Alex Avich 69 (5c), Evgeniy Ayupov 21 (3a), Kitch Bain 50 (i), Marilyn Barbone 93 (1b), Boris15 93 (8b), Borodaev 69 (3b), Robyn Butler 30br, Tony Campbell 45 (3b), ckchiu 74 (i), Clearviewstock 98 (a), Dusty Cline 14 (b), HD Connelly 50 (c), Coprid 69 (3c), Cheryl E. Davis 62 (h), Dreamframer 21t (5a), 21t (5b), Sebastian Duda 45 (8a), Dusan964 21 (4a), 21 (4b), 45 (3c), eAilsa 54 (glass), Elenamiv 14 (h), Elnur 93 (5b), Erissona 14 (e), Stephen Finn 74 (e), Fivespots 45 (3a), Gelpi 11l, 13l, 35l, 69 (1c), 105 (4b), Gemphotography 98 (d), R. Gino Santa Maria 35r, Mandy Godbehear 45 (2a), goldenangel 74 (d), Maksym Gorpenyuk 45 (4a), Grafica 33 (4a), Gresei 86 (h), Grocap 50 (d), Iwona Grodzka 69 (5b), Gwoeii 62 (g), Scott Hales 93 (7b), Peter Hansen 45 (2c), Margo Harrison 62 (j), Hifashion 69 (4a), Margrit Hirsch 86 (b), Icyimage 105 (2b), Karlova Irina 69 (1b), Tischenko Irina 50 (e), 74 (h), Eric Isselée 38 (g), 38 (j), 45 (4c), 45 (6c), 45 (7a), 58tr, J.D.S. 74 (j), Junker 45 (1b), Olga Kadroff 62 (d), Evgeny Karandaev 89 (4), Karkas 62 (c), 69 (3a), 69 (4c), 69 (5a), Judy Kennamer 33 (1b), khz 89 (5), Kirsanov 45 (4b), Igor Kisselev 62 (e), Alexandr Kolupayev 38 (i), Iurii Konoval 62 (b), Dmitry Kosterev 102r, Vasiliy Koval 45 (5c), 45 (7b), Viachaslau Kraskouski 93 (6b), Lasse Kristensen 50 (f), Kirill Kurashov 69 (1a), Edgaras Kurauskas 50 (h), Goran Kuzmanovski 93 (3a), Wolfe Larry 89 (1), Henrik Larsson 21t (5c), 21b (5b), Chris Leachman 11r, David Lee 38 (b), Lepas 62 (a), 86 (c), 93 (7a), Joshua Lewis 45 (5b), luSh 86 (f), markrhiggins 30tl, Maska 10, Lorelyn Medina 33 (2a), MikLav 98 (b), Karam Miri 50 (a), 50 (j), Mitya 21 (4c), Juriah Mosin 61r, Nadezda 69 (2c), Naluwan 85r, Nattika 93 (5a), 93 (8a), Nikkytok 14 (g), ODM Studio 38 (f), Oksix 93 (4b), Zhuchkova Olena 47tl, Optimarc 93 (3b), 93 (4a), Padal 33 (3b), Varina and Jay Patel 45 (6a), Anita Patterson Peppers 45 (2b), Paulaphoto 33 (2b), 61l, 105 (3a), Lobke Peers 45 (1a), Thomas M Perkins 85l, Photocrea 93 (1a), Picamaniac 89 (2), pix2go 38 (a), Rainer Plendl 105 (4a), Olga Popova 69 (6b), Rook76 93 (2b), Ruzanna 50 (g), s_oleg 45 (5a), Sarah2 21 (3b), Sergio Schnitzler 69 (6a), Nata Sdobnikova 69 (2a), SF Photo 45 (8b), Serhiy Shullye 86 (g), Roman Sigaev 45 (1c), Viorel Sima 38 (c), Worakit Sirijinda 69 (4b), Smit 21 (3c), 38 (e), 89 (3), Perov Stanislav 69 (2b), Studio Online 21b (5c), Tatniz 62 (i), Christophe Testi 62 (f), Kiselev Andrey Valerevich 105 (1a), Martin Valigursky 38 (d), Liz Van Steenburgh 86 (a), Vankad 89 (7), Valentyn Volkov 86 (e), 89 (6), 93 (2a), 93 (6a), George Vollmy 102l, Voylodyon 14 (f), Michael Wesemann 38 (h), Ivonne Wierink 50 (b), Jamie Wilson 30tr, Wlg 74 (a), Senol Yaman 69 (6c), Yasonya 86 (d), Otna Ydur 89 (8), Jess Yu 74 (c), Shawn Zhan 74 (b), Aleksandar Zoric 105 (1b); Thinkstock: Hemera 58tl, iStockphoto 46l, 47 (spider), 95tl, and liquidlibrary 95bl.

All other images © Pearson Education Limited

Contents

Scope and sequence

Welcome

Vocabulary	**Numbers:** twenty-one to fifty **Months of the year:** January, February, March, April, May, June, July, August, September, October, November, December
Structures	What's your favorite day? My favorite day is Sunday. When were you born? I was born in January. Were you born in May? Yes, I was. / No, I wasn't. I was born in June.

1 Nature

Vocabulary	**Nature:** animal, sun, rock, pond, birds, flowers, insects, mushrooms, clouds, trees, ants, worms, spiders, butterflies, roses, rainbow, wind, sky	**Values:** Play outside. Play safe.
Structures	How many animals are there? There's one purple animal. How many birds are there? There are two blue birds. There are some ants. / There aren't any ants. Are there any ants? Yes, there are. / No, there aren't. Is there a rainbow? Yes, there is. / No, there isn't. Is there any wind? Yes, there's some wind. / No, there isn't any wind.	**Cross-curricular:** **Math:** Plus, minus, equals **Phonics:** air, ear fair, pair, hair, chair, tear, year, hear, near

2 Me

Vocabulary	**Physical characteristics:** a small nose, a black mustache, a short beard, thick eyebrows, brown eyes, small glasses, red hair, gray hair, blond hair, a round chin, a strong chest, a flat stomach, broad shoulders, strong arms, long eyelashes, a long neck, short fingernails	**Values:** Have good habits. Keep clean and healthy.
Structures	I have a small nose. I don't have thick eyebrows. He/She has a small nose. He/She doesn't have thick eyebrows. Do you have a round chin? Yes, I do. / No, I don't. Does he/she have broad shoulders? Yes, he/she does. / No, he/she doesn't.	**Cross-curricular:** **Science:** Wild animals **Phonics:** ay, er say, day, way, play, dinner, summer, hammer, letter

3 Pets

Vocabulary	**Animal body parts:** a tail, a beak, wings, feathers, claws, fins, paws, whiskers, skin, fur **Animal characteristics:** spotted fur, striped fur, soft fur, smooth skin, a hard shell, sharp claws **Adjectives:** cute, scary, fast, slow	**Values:** Take care of your pet. **Cross-curricular:** **Science:** Animal life cycles
Structures	What does it look like? It has a tail. It doesn't have wings. What do they look like? They have tails. They don't have wings. Do you have a dog? Yes, I do. It's cute. / No, I don't. Does it have spotted fur? Yes, it does. / No, it doesn't.	**Phonics:** ea, oi eat, tea, leaf, peach, oil, coin, join, foil

4 Home

Vocabulary	**Furnishings:** plant, mirror, picture, shower, closet, garbage can **Prepositions:** below, above, behind, in front of, next to **Household items:** computer, cupboard, toothbrush, comb, broom, plates, pots, pans, towels, blankets	**Values:** Help at home. **Cross-curricular:** **Art:** Mosaics
Structures	There's a plant in the living room. There are two plants in the living room. The plant is below the mirror. / It's below the mirror. The plants are below the mirror. / They're below the mirror. Is the computer in the bedroom? Yes, it is. / No, it isn't. It's in the living room. Are the plates in the cupboard? Yes, they are. / No, they aren't. They're in the sink.	**Phonics:** a_e, i_e, o_e cake, wave, shape, time, dive, like, bone, home, note

5 Clothes

Vocabulary	Clothing: a baseball cap, a belt, a sweatshirt, a sweatsuit, a blouse, a uniform, a polo shirt, shorts, sandals, slippers, scarf, beanie, ski jacket, wool sweater, tights, hiking boots Material/style: leather, fancy, plain, colorful
Structures	What are you wearing? I'm wearing a baseball cap/shorts. What's he/she wearing? He's/She's wearing a baseball cap/shorts. Are you wearing a baseball cap/shorts? Yes, I am. / No, I'm not. Is he/she wearing a baseball cap/shorts? Yes, he/she is. / No, he/she isn't. This is my favorite scarf. These are my favorite tights. I love my scarf/tights.

Values: Be polite.

Cross-curricular:
Social science: Household chores

Phonics: sc, sk, sm, sn, sp, squ, st, sw
scarf, skate, smell, snip, spoon, squid, star, swim

6 Sports

Vocabulary	Abilities: run, ride a bike, catch a ball, play soccer, play baseball, play tennis, play basketball, do taekwondo Sports facilities: gym, baseball field, basketball court, running track, stadium, skating rink, ski slope, bowling alley, beach, swimming pool
Structures	I can run and ride a bike. I can run but I can't ride a bike. Can he/she run? Yes, he/she can. / No, he/she can't. I/He/She was at the gym. I/He/She wasn't at the gym. I/He/She was at the baseball field.

Values: Be active. Exercise every day.

Cross-curricular:
Health: Exercise

Phonics: bl, fl, gl, pl, sl
black, flag, float, glass, plum, plate, slip, sleep

7 Food

Vocabulary	Fruit / Vegetables: peas, mangoes, carrots, cucumbers, plums, oranges, peaches, potatoes, tomatoes, strawberries, broccoli, lettuce, spinach, cabbage, pears, apricots, avocadoes, cherries
Structures	Do you like peas? Yes, I do. / No, I don't. Does he/she like peas? Yes, he/she does. / No, he/she doesn't. Is there any broccoli? Yes, there is. / No, there isn't. Are there any pears? Yes, there are. / No, there aren't.

Values: Stay healthy. Eat more fruit and vegetables.

Cross-curricular:
Science: Food pyramid

Phonics: br, cr, dr, fr, gr, pr, str, tr
brown, crab, drop, frog, green, press, string, train

8 Things we do

Vocabulary	Actions: sleeping, reading, eating, drinking, cleaning, walking, dancing, doing homework, listening to music, making a machine, singing, playing the piano, playing the violin, playing the trumpet, playing the flute Adverbs of manner: quietly, loudly, quickly, slowly, terribly
Structures	What are you doing? I'm sleeping. What are they doing? They're sleeping. What's he/she doing? He's/She's sleeping. Are you singing? Yes, I am. / No, I'm not. Is he/she singing? Yes, he/she is. / No, he/she isn't. Is he/she singing quietly? Yes, he/she. / No, he/she isn't. He's/She's singing loudly.

Values: Learn new things. Develop your talents.

Cross-curricular:
Science: Flying machines

Phonics: ft, mp, nd, nt, sk, sp, st
left, bump, hand, wind, paint, ask, wisp, nest

Welcome

Where are we, Professor Bloom?

1

It's Space Island.

Wow! It's great!

2

Professor, I'm scared!

3

Don't worry. It's nice. It's sunny!

4

Look! Two suns!

5

Oh!!!

SPLOS!

21 twenty-one	**22** twenty-two	**23** twenty-three	**24** twenty-four	**25** twenty-five
26 twenty-six	**27** twenty-seven	**28** twenty-eight	**29** twenty-nine	**30** thirty
31 thirty-one	**32** thirty-two	**33** thirty-three	**34** thirty-four	**35** thirty-five
36 thirty-six	**37** thirty-seven	**38** thirty-eight	**39** thirty-nine	**40** forty
41 forty-one	**42** forty-two	**43** forty-three	**44** forty-four	**45** forty-five
46 forty-six	**47** forty-seven	**48** forty-eight	**49** forty-nine	**50** fifty

4 A:06 **Listen and circle.**

a twenty-six / twenty-seven / twenty-eight

b thirty-two / thirty-four / thirty-nine

c forty-one / forty-three / forty-five

d twenty-three / thirty-three / forty-three

e twenty-seven / thirty-seven / forty-seven

5 **Write five numbers. Then ask and answer.**

> Let me guess.
> Is it 33?

> No, it isn't. My turn.

6 A:07-08 **Sing.**

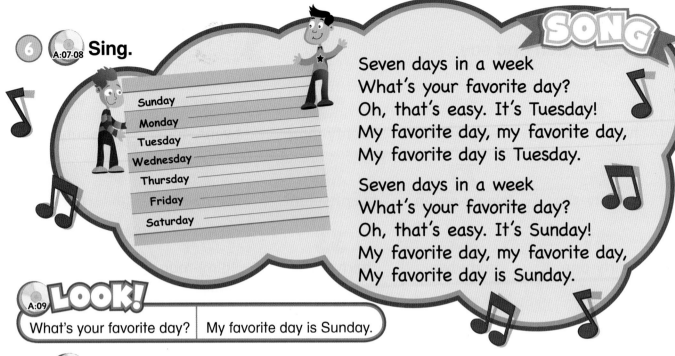

Seven days in a week
What's your favorite day?
Oh, that's easy. It's Tuesday!
My favorite day, my favorite day,
My favorite day is Tuesday.

Seven days in a week
What's your favorite day?
Oh, that's easy. It's Sunday!
My favorite day, my favorite day,
My favorite day is Sunday.

A:09 **LOOK!**

| What's your favorite day? | My favorite day is Sunday. |

7 A:10 **Listen and circle.**

1 Mark
My favorite day is (Monday / Tuesday / Wednesday).

2 Tina
My favorite day is (Thursday / Friday / Saturday).

3 Sam
My favorite day is (Saturday / Sunday / Monday).

8 **Check (✓). Then ask, answer, and check (✓).**

What's your favorite day?

My favorite day is Friday.

	Me	(Friend 1)	(Friend 2)	(Friend 3)
Monday				
Tuesday				
Wednesday				
Thursday				
Friday				
Saturday				
Sunday				

Favorite day of the week

9 **Listen and say. Then listen and number.**

January	February	March	April
May	June	July	August
September	October	November	December

10 **Listen and circle.**

1 He was born in (January / February / March / April).

2 She was born in (May / June / July / August).

3  They were born in (September / October / November / December).

11 **Check (✓). Then ask, answer, and check (✓).**

	Me	_____ (Friend 1)	_____ (Friend 2)	_____ (Friend 3)
January				
February				
March				
April				
May				
June				
July				
August				
September				
October				
November				
December				

When were you born?

I was born in July.

1 A:15 Listen.

2 A:16 **Listen and say.**

3 A:17 **Listen and number.**

a animal

b sun

c rock

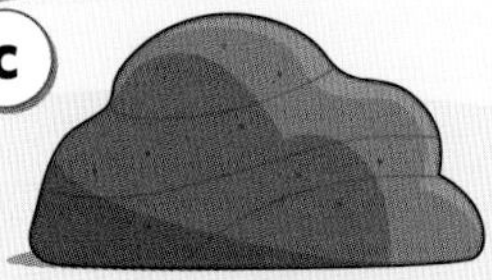

d pond

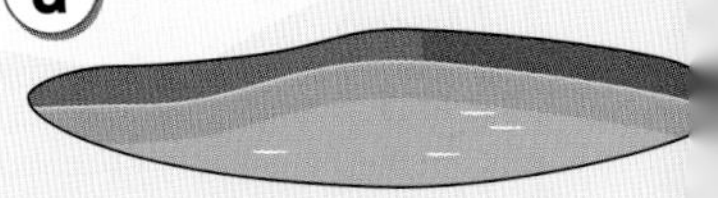

f flowers

g insects

h mushrooms

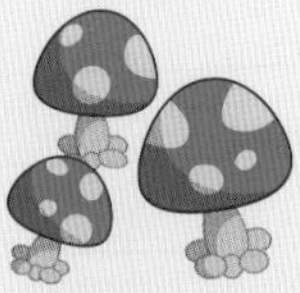

i clouds

4 A:18-19 **Listen and chant.** (See page 112.)

A:20 **LOOK!**

How many animals are there?	There's one purple animal.
How many birds are there?	There are two blue birds.

5 **Look at the scene. Count, write, and check (✓). Then ask and answer.**

			There is	There are
1		____	☐	☐
2		____	☐	☐
3		____	☐	☐
4		____	☐	☐

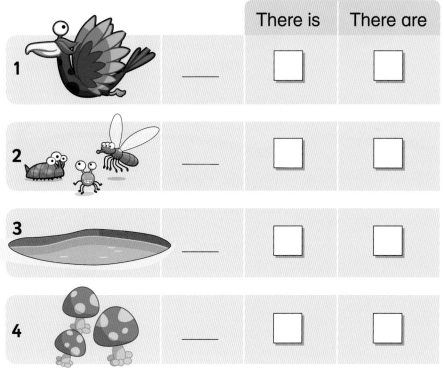

How many birds are there?

There are two birds.

e **birds**

j **trees**

A:21 Quest

6 A:22 **Listen and say.**

a ants

b worms

c spiders

d butterflies

e roses

f rainbow

g wind

h sky

7 A:23-24 **Listen and stick. Then sing.**

SONG

How many, how many are there?

There are seven _____.

There are six spiders.

There are five _____.

Seven, six, five!

Stamp, stamp, stamp!

Stamp, stamp, stamp, stamp, stamp!

How many, how many are there?

There are four _____.

There are three butterflies.

There are two _____.

Four, three, two!

Clap, clap, clap!

Clap, clap, clap, clap, clap!

How many rainbows are there?

There's one rainbow,

Only one rainbow

Up in the _____.

Jump, jump, run!

Jump, jump, run, jump, run!

Stick

LOOK!

A:25

There are some ants.	There aren't any ants.
Are there any ants?	Yes, there are. / No, there aren't.
Is there a rainbow?	Yes, there is. / No, there isn't.
Is there any wind?	Yes, there's some wind. / No, there isn't any wind.

8 A:26 **Listen and circle the correct screen. Then ask and answer.**

9 **Look at the South screen in Activity 8. Write.**

A : _____ trees?

B : _____, _____.

A : _____ rain?

B : _____, _____. _____ a rainbow.

A : _____ insects?

B : _____, _____. _____ birds.

11 **Where is Hoopla in the story? Discuss your answers.**

12 Match.

1 The aliens' names are   Hip and Hop's mushrooms.

2 Harry counts   the ball to Harry.

3 Rose likes   to Hoopla.

4 Hip says, "This isn't   thirty mushrooms.

5 Hoopla gives   a mushroom."

6 Harry says thanks   Hip and Hop.

 13 Role-play the story.

 14 Write Y = Yes or N = No.
Then ask and answer.

 VALUES

Play outside. Play safe.

Me ☐ My friend ☐

Play in the playground.

Me ☐ My friend ☐

Play in the streets.

Me ☐ My friend ☐

Play at night.

Me ☐ My friend ☐

Play by yourself.

Me ☐ My friend ☐

Play with friends.

Me ☐ My friend ☐

Play in the hot sun.

Do you play in the playground?

Yes, I do.

HOME-SCHOOL LINK

Think of a way to play safe when you are outside. Draw a picture. Show your family.

15  **Count and write. Then listen and check your answers.**

+ (plus) **– (minus)** **= (equals)**

a   **+**   **=** ☐

b **–**   **=** ☐

c   **+**   **=** ☐

d   **–**   **=** ☐

16 **Read the number riddles. Then write the answer.**

1  **+**

I'm the number of legs on three birds, plus the number of legs on a horse. What number am I? ☐

2 I'm the number of legs on two insects, minus the number of legs on a cat. What number am I? ☐

THINK!

A **bi**ped animal has <u>two</u> legs.
A **quadru**ped animal has <u>four</u> legs.

1 Are humans quadrupeds or bipeds?
2 Name two bipeds and two quadrupeds.

MINI-PROJECT Write a number riddle.

17 A:29 **Listen.**

1 air   ## 2 ear

18 A:30 **Listen, point, and say.**

19 A:31 **Listen and blend the sounds.**

1   f – air   fair   2   p – air   pair

3   h – air   hair   4   ch – air   chair

5   t – ear   tear   6   y – ear   year

7   h – ear   hear   8   n – ear   near

20 **Underline *air* and *ear*. Read the sentences aloud.**

1   This girl has long hair.   2   Sit down on the chair.

3   I can hear with my ear.   4   A pair is near the chair.

 **Play.**

■ How many ... are there?   □ Is/Are there any ...?

Student A

Start   Finish

... spiders?

... butterflies?

... pond?

... rainbow?

Finish   Start

Student B

How to play

1 Student A starts from the top of the board and Student B starts from the bottom. Each student has a coin as a counter.

2 Students play rock-paper-scissors. Using the coin, the winner is the first one to move and answer the question.

3 Students take turns moving from stone to stone and asking and answering questions. If the answer is wrong, the student loses a turn.

4 The student who reaches the "Finish" space first wins.

5 Students change places and play again.

22 A:32 **Listen and check (✓) or write.**

1 five animals ☐

one animal ☐

two animals ☐

2 five ants ☐

six ants ☐

seven ants ☐

3

a ☐   b ☐   c ☐

4 a ☐   b ☐   c ☐

5 a ☐   b ☐   c ☐
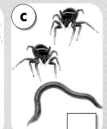

6 a ☐   b ☐   c ☐

7 a ☐   b ☐

8 a ☐   b ☐

9 How many _____? _____.

10 _____? Yes, there _____.

 I can describe nature. ☐

I can solve math problems. ☐

TEACHER

Now go to Space Island.

Wider world 1
Birthdays around the world

1 (A:33) **Listen and read.**

Hi, I'm Lucy. I'm from the United States. Today is my birthday. I'm nine. Look at my birthday cake. There are nine candles. My friends and family sing "Happy birthday" and I blow out the candles. I love birthdays!

candle

cake

1

2

piñata

My name's Diego and I'm eight. I'm from Mexico. Look! It's my birthday party. There's a big *piñata* with candy inside. They fall down and we love them.

3

Hello, I'm Yoon-ji and I'm from Korea. I'm eight today. For my birthday I have a big breakfast in the morning with seaweed soup and *banchan*. These are side dishes. Yum!

banchan

seaweed soup

2 Write T = True or F = False.

1 Diego is nine.

2 Lucy has a cake with nine candles.

3 Diego has a *piñata*.

4 Yoon-ji likes seaweed soup.

3 Ask and answer.

1 How old are you?
2 Is there a cake at your birthday party?
3 Are there candles?
4 Are there any gifts?
5 Is there any candy?

1 (A:34) **Listen.**

Peter   Jane

2 (A:35) **Listen and say.**   **3** (A:36) **Listen and number.**

a a small nose

b a black mustache

c a short beard

d thick eyebrows

f small glasses

g red hair

h gray hair

4 A:37-38 **Listen and chant.** (See page 112.)

 A:39 **LOOK!**

I	have	a small nose.
	don't have	thick eyebrows.
He She	has	
	doesn't have	

5 **Look at the scene and circle. Then say.**

1 Mom has (blond hair / red hair).
She (has / doesn't have) glasses.

2 Grandpa has (green eyes / brown eyes).
He has (brown hair / gray hair).

3 I'm Peter. I have (small glasses / a small nose).
I (have / don't have) thick eyebrows.

4 Dad has (a black mustache / small glasses)
and (a short beard / brown eyes).

He has red hair. He doesn't have glasses.

Peter!

e brown eyes

i blond hair

A:40

6 (A:41) **Listen and say.**

a a round chin

d broad shoulders

f long eyelashes

g a long neck

b a strong chest

e strong arms

c a flat stomach

h short fingernails

7 (A:42-43) **Listen and circle. Then sing.**

Who am I? Who am I? Who am I?

Do you have (a strong chest / strong legs)?

Yes, I do. Yes, I do. Yes, I do.

Do you have (a long neck / a round chin)? Yes, I do.

Do you have (a long neck / a short neck)?

Yes, I do. Yes, I do. Yes, I do.

Do you have (blond hair / long eyelashes)? Yes, I do.

Do you have (a strong chest / strong arms)?

No, I don't. No, I don't. No, I don't.

Do you have (broad shoulders / a small nose)? Yes, I do.

Who am I? Who am I? Who am I?

A:44 LOOK!

Do you	have	a round chin? broad shoulders?	Yes, I do.
			No, I don't.
Does he/she			Yes, he/she does.
			No, he/she doesn't.

8 A:45 **Listen and number. Then ask and answer.**

a

Arisu

b

Paulo

c

Rose

Picture B. Does he have a round chin?

Yes, he does.

9 **Look at Activity 8 and check (✓).**

		Arisu	Paulo	Rose
1	Who has strong arms?	☐	☐	☐
2	Who has broad shoulders?	☐	☐	☐
3	Who has a round chin?	☐	☐	☐
4	Who has long eyelashes?	☐	☐	☐
5	Who has a flat stomach?	☐	☐	☐

  Is Hip's new friend an alien or a monster? Discuss your answers.

28 Consolidation

Listen and circle.

1 (a)   (b)

2 (a)   (b)

3   He has (two eyes /

twenty legs).

4   Yes, he does. /

No, he doesn't.

Role-play the story.

**Write Y = Yes or N = No.
Then ask and answer.**

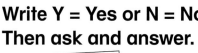 **VALUES**

Have good habits.
Keep clean and healthy.

①

Me ☐ My friend ☐

Keep your fingernails short.

②

Me ☐ My friend ☐

Brush your teeth every day.

③

Me ☐ My friend ☐

Take a bath or shower every day.

④

Me ☐ My friend ☐

Wash your hands before and after eating.

⑤

Me ☐ My friend ☐

Eat a lot of vegetables.

⑥

Me ☐ My friend ☐

Cover your mouth when coughing.

Do you keep your fingernails short?   Yes, I do.

HOME-SCHOOL LINK

Write three things you can do to keep your body clean. Show your family.

 PARENT

15 A:48 **Read and stick.**

Australian animals

1

2

3

marsupial

The kangaroo has a pouch and a big body. It has two long legs and two short arms. It has a small head and a short neck. It has big ears and small eyes.

Stick

reptile

This is a blind snake. It isn't very long. It has a small round head. It has a small mouth and two very small eyes. It can't see!

bird

The emu has long feathers and a big body. It has two long legs and a small head. It has a long neck and big eyes.

16 A:49 **Listen and circle T = True or F = False.**

1 T / F **2** T / F **3** T / F **4** T / F **5** T / F **6** T / F

17 **Choose an animal and describe it to your friend.**

koala

big ears

small eyes

fur

big nose

pouch

The koala has ....

small eyes

wombat

round nose

brown fur

little legs

The wombat has ....

THINK!

Can you find marsupials in your country?

MINI-PROJECT

Write about an animal from your country.

SOUNDS FUN!

18  **Listen.**

1 ay   **2 er**

19 (A:51) **Listen, point, and say.**

20 (A:52) **Listen and blend the sounds.**

1 s – ay   say   **2** d – ay   day

3 w – ay   way   **4** p – l – ay   play

5 d – i – nn – er   dinner   **6** s – u – mm – er   summer

7 h – a – mm – er   hammer   **8** l – e – tt – er   letter

21 **Underline *ay* and *er*. Read the sentences aloud.**

1 We want fish for dinner.

2 A letter is in the mailbox.

3 We play all day in the summer.

4 I play with my toy hammer.

HAVE FUN!

1 Jonas

2 Jenny

3 Bill

4 Susan

5 Marco

6 David

7 Alice

8 Joe

9 Peter

10 Lucy

11 Adam

12 Rosie

13 Jack

14 Julie

15 Sally

16 Betty

Do you have brown hair? Yes, I do.

Do you have thick eyebrows? Yes, I do.

Are you Bill? Yes!

Guess!

23 **Listen and check (✓) or write.**

1 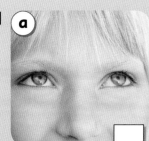 **a** | **b**   **2**  **a** | **b**

3  **a** | **b**   **4**  **a** | **b**

5  **a** | **b** | **c**   **6** 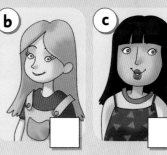 **a** | **b** | **c**

7  **a** | **b**   **8**  **a** | **b**

9 Do _____ have _____? _____

10 Does she _____? _____

I can describe physical appearance. ☐
I can identify some wild animals from Australia. ☐

Now go to Space Island.

Review Units 1 and 2

Play.

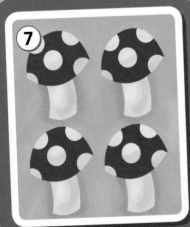

He has blond hair and blue eyes.

It's Number 12.

3 Pets

1 **A:54** Listen.

2 **A:55** Listen and say.　　3 **A:56** Listen and number.

a

a tail

b
a beak

c
wings

d
feathers

f
fins

g
paws

h
whiskers

i
skin

A:59 **LOOK!**

What	does it	look like?
	do they	
It	has	a tail.
	doesn't have	wings.
They	have	tails.
	don't have	wings.

5 **Circle. Then ask and answer.**

1 It has big eyes.
It doesn't have legs.

2 It has two eyes.
It has wings.

3 It has a tail. It doesn't
have fins.

4 It has whiskers. It has
long ears.

e

claws

j

fur

 A:60
Quest

What does it look like?

It's green.
It has four legs
and big eyes.

It's a frog.

6 (A:61) **Listen and say.**

a spotted fur

b striped fur

c soft fur

d smooth skin

e a hard shell

f sharp claws

g cute

h scary

i fast

j slow

7 (A:62-63) **Listen and write. Then sing.**

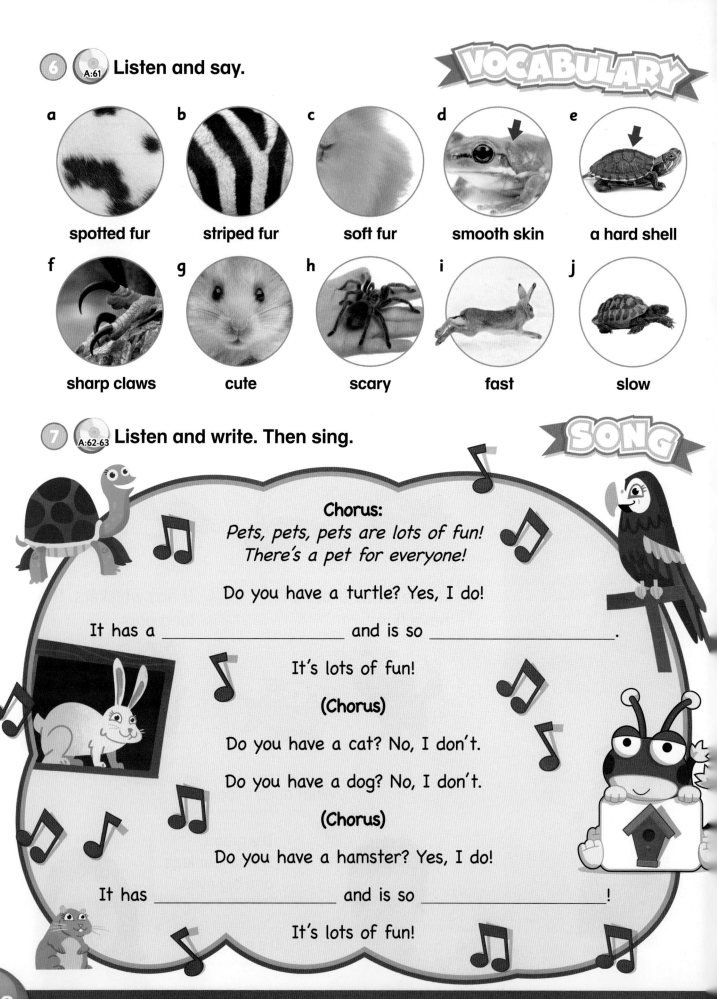

Chorus:
Pets, pets, pets are lots of fun!
There's a pet for everyone!

Do you have a turtle? Yes, I do!

It has a _____ and is so _____.

It's lots of fun!

(Chorus)

Do you have a cat? No, I don't.

Do you have a dog? No, I don't.

(Chorus)

Do you have a hamster? Yes, I do!

It has _____ and is so _____!

It's lots of fun!

Animal characteristics

| Do you have a dog? | Yes, I do. It's cute. | Does it have spotted fur? | Yes, it does. |
| | No, I don't. | | No, it doesn't. |

8 Choose a pet. Ask and answer.

1

paws, tail, claws, spotted fur

2

hard shell, slow, fun

3

beak, feathers, wings, fast

4

soft fur, short tail, cute, fast

5

fins, clean

6

smooth skin, scary

My pet has wings. It's fast.

Do you have a bird?

Yes, I do.

9 Write.

 SKILLS

My pet

Animal: tarantula
Name: Boris
Home: Arizona
Age: 3 years old
Color: brown
Legs: 8 legs, striped fur
Food: insects

Hi. I'm Alex and I have a pet. It's a
_____ and it's from Arizona.
It's _____ old.
It's brown. It doesn't have a tail. It has eight
_____ and short, striped fur.
It likes to eat _____.
Some people say it's scary.
I say it's cute and very smart.
I love my pet tarantula.

Listen and read.

 What animals can you find in the story? Discuss your answers.

 **Circle.**

1 　Is it a frog? 　　　　　　　a　Yes, it is. / No, it isn't.

　　　　　　　Does it have four legs? 　b　Yes, it does. / No, it doesn't.

2 　Does it have legs? 　　　　a　Yes, it does. / No, it doesn't.

　　　　　　　Does it have fins? 　　　b　Yes, it does. / No, it doesn't.

3 　Does it have spotted skin? 　a　Yes, it does. / No, it doesn't.

　　　　　　　Is it green? 　　　　　b　Yes, it is. / No, it isn't.

13 **Role-play the story.**

14 **Write Y = Yes or N = No.**
Then ask and answer.

VALUES

Take care of your pet.

1

Me ☐ My friend ☐

Feed your pet every day.

2

Me ☐ My friend ☐

Give your pet fresh water.

3

Me ☐ My friend ☐

Take your pet to the vet.

4

Me ☐ My friend ☐

Keep your pet clean.

5

Me ☐ My friend ☐

Give your pet exercise.

6

Me ☐ My friend ☐

Clean your pet's home.

Do you feed your pet every day?

Yes, I do.

HOME-SCHOOL LINK

Draw your dream pet. Show your family.

15 A:66 **Read and stick.**

1 First, there are small eggs.
2 Next, there are caterpillars. They have many legs and big eyes.
3 Then, there are cocoons. Cocoons are cases around the caterpillars' bodies.

4 Finally, there are butterflies. What do they look like? They have wings with many colors. They can be striped or spotted.

eggs   **caterpillars**   **cocoons**   **butterflies**

16 A:67 **Read. Then write.**

THINK!

The picture on this page is a *diagram*. It helps you understand information better. Find other diagrams in this book.

1
First, there are small eggs in the water.

3
Then the tadpoles are big. They have two legs now and long tails. They can swim fast.

2
Then there are small tadpoles. They have long tails. They don't have legs.

4
Finally, there are young frogs. They have four legs now. They have big eyes and big mouths. They can jump.

1 Where are the eggs? They're _____.

2 Do small tadpoles have short tails?
No, they have _____.

3 Do big tadpoles have four legs? No, they have _____.

4 What can frogs do? They _____.

MINI-
PROJECT
Make a diagram for the life cycle of a snake.

17 A:68 **Listen.**

1 # ea

2 # oi

18 A:69 **Listen, point, and say.**

19 A:70 **Listen and blend the sounds.**

1 ea – t eat
2 t – ea tea
3 l – ea – f leaf
4 p – ea – ch peach
5 oi – l oil
6 c – oi – n coin
7 j – oi – n join
8 f – oi – l foil

20 **Underline _ea_ and _oi_. Read the sentences aloud.**

1 I have a silver coin.

2 Eat a peach.

3 Put oil on the foil.

4 Join me for leaf tea.

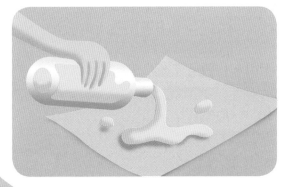

Draw or write. Then play.

 HAVE FUN!

My house

backyard

bathroom	bedroom 2
dining room	kitchen
bedroom 1	living room

garden

My friend's house

backyard

bathroom	bedroom 2
dining room	kitchen
bedroom 1	living room

garden

Do you have a pet in the bathroom? — Yes, I do.

Does it have legs? — No, it doesn't.

Is it green? — Yes, it is.

Is it a snake? — Yes!

 Guess!

Listen and check (✓) or write.

1 a  □ b  □ c  □   **2** a  □ b  □ c  □

3 a 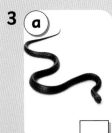 □ b  □ c  □   **4** a  □ b  □ c  □

5 a  □ b  □ c  □   **6** a  □ b  □ c 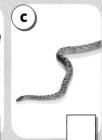 □

7 a  □ b  □   **8** a  □ b  □

9 _____ a pet? _____, _____.

10 _____ have soft fur? _____, _____.

 I can talk and write about pets. □
I can understand and make diagrams. □

Now go to Space Island.

Wider world 2

Do you like pets?

1 🔘 A:72 **Listen and read.**

My name's Dagang. I'm from China. I have a pet rabbit. His name is Baobao. He's white and he has long ears. His fur is very soft. He doesn't like cheese or pizza. He likes apples and salad. I love my pet rabbit.

My name's Rika and I'm from Japan. I have a pet hamster. Her name is Momo. She's two years old. She has a small tail and a small head. She likes apples and nuts and her hamster wheel. She's so cute. I love hamsters!

2 ✏️ **Match.**

1 turtle		fish and cheese
2 rabbit		apples and nuts
3 hamster		apples and eggs
4 cat		apples and salad

3

I'm Pedro and I'm from Colombia. I have a pet cat. Her name is Olly and she's nine years old. She's white. She likes fish and cheese, but she doesn't like fruit. I love Olly.

4

I'm Jane and I'm from Australia. I have a pet turtle. His name is Bruno. He has a small head and four strong legs. He's 15 years old. He has a very hard shell. He's big and he likes apples and eggs.

3 **Ask and answer.**

parrot   iguana   duck   spider

1   Do you like these pets?
2   Why do you like them?
3   What's your favorite pet?

1 B:02 **Listen.**

2 B:03 **Listen and say.**

3 B:04 **Listen and number.**

a **plant**

b **mirror**

c **picture**

d **shower**

e **closet**

g **below**

h **above**

i **behind**

j **in front of**

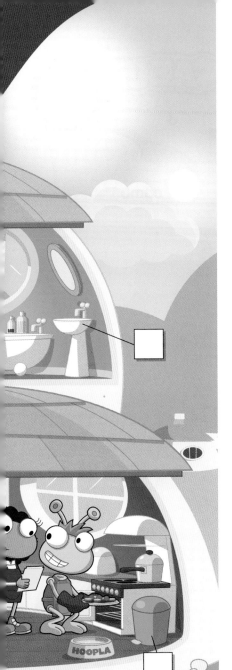

4 B:05-06 **Listen and chant.** (See page 112.)

B:07 LOOK!

There's a plant	in the living room.
There are two plants	
The plant is / It's	below the mirror.
The plants are / They're	

5 B:08 **Listen and circle the things you hear. Then say.**

f
garbage can

k
next to

B:09
Quest

There's a computer on the table.

6 B:10 **Listen and say.**

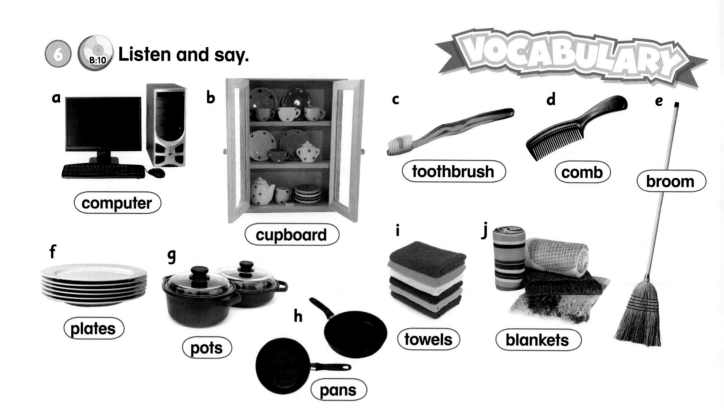

a **computer**

b **cupboard**

c **toothbrush**

d **comb**

e **broom**

f **plates**

g **pots**

h **pans**

i **towels**

j **blankets**

7 B:11-12 **Listen and circle. Then sing.**

Chorus:
Messy house, messy rooms everywhere.
With messy things here, and messy things there.
Behind, below, above, there.
Clean up, clean up everywhere.

Where are the (/)?
Are they on the shelf? No, they aren't!
They're next to the chair.
(Chorus)

Where's the (/)?
Is it above the sink? No, it isn't!
It's under the plates.
(Chorus)

Where are the (/)?
Are they in the closet? No, they aren't!
They're behind the plant.

  LOOK!

B:13

Is the computer in the bedroom?	Yes, it is.	Are the plates in the cupboard?	Yes, they are.
	No, it isn't. It's in the living room.		No, they aren't. They're in the sink.

8 **Choose two rooms and stick. Then say.**

My favorite room is the bathroom. There's a telephone next to the mirror!

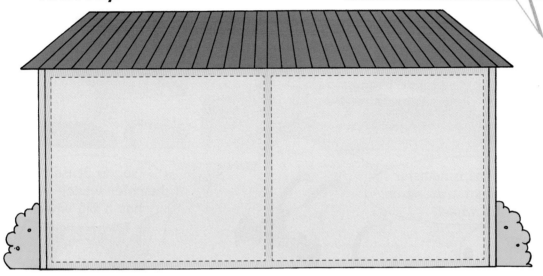

Stick

9 **Read. Then listen and write.**

B:14-15

SKILLS

My best friend is coming to my house! I have a great new bed in my bedroom for her. It's next to the closet. It's fantastic. It's green and there's a frog on it! Well, there's a picture of a frog. It's cool! The frog is in the pool. Do you like it?

1 <u>No, she isn't</u>. She's in the _____.

2 _____, she _____.

3 _____, _____. It's _____ the _____.

4 It's _____ the _____ .

10 **B:16** **Listen and read.**

 11 **Is Hoopla a hamster? Discuss your answers.**

12 (B:17) **Listen and check (✓).**

1 (a)  (b) ☐

2 (a) 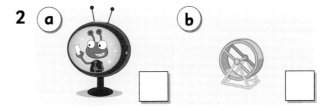 (b) ☐

3 (a)  (b) ☐

4 (a) It's next to the table. ☐
  (b) It's behind the table. ☐
  (c) It's under the table. ☐

13 Role-play the story.

14 Write Y = Yes or N = No.
Then ask and answer.

VALUES
Help at home.

1
Me ☐ My friend ☐
Sweep the floor.

2
Me ☐ My friend ☐
Put away your toys.

3
Me ☐ My friend ☐
Dust the shelves.

4
Me ☐ My friend ☐
Dry the dishes.

5
Me ☐ My friend ☐
Take out the garbage.

6
Me ☐ My friend ☐
Hang up your clothes.

Do you sweep the floor?

Yes, I do.

HOME-SCHOOL LINK
Clean your room. Show your family.

15 **B:18-19** **Read. Then listen and circle or write.**

This is a mosaic. It is a picture that has small tiles, stones, or glass. It has squares, circles, rectangles, and triangles in different colors. There are mosaics on floors and on walls. They are very beautiful. Do you like mosaics?

tiles

stones

glass

1 Yes, they are. / No, they aren't.

2 Yes, there are. / No, there aren't.

3 (Yes / No). It's a _____ of a _____.

16 **Count the shapes and write.**

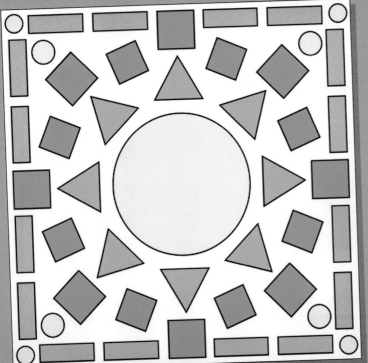

THINK!

What other things can be used to make mosaics?

1 How many triangles are there? ☐

2 How many squares are there? ☐

3 How many circles are there? ☐

4 How many rectangles are there? ☐

MINI-**PROJECT**

Draw a mosaic of your favorite animal.

SOUNDS FUN!

17 **Listen.**

1 a_e   **2** i_e   **3** o_e

18 **Listen, point, and say.**

19 **Listen and blend the sounds.**

1 c – a – ke cake   **2** w – a – ve wave

3 sh – a – pe shape   **4** t – i – me time

5 d – i – ve dive   **6** l – i – ke like

7 b – o – ne bone   **8** h – o – me home

9 n – o – te note

20 **Underline** *a_e*, *i_e*, **and** *o_e*. **Read the sentences aloud.**

1 The dog has a bone.   **2** I like cake!

3 Dive under the wave.   **4** It's time to go home.

Student A

bathroom

living room

dining room

kitchen

bedroom

bedroom

front yard

Student B

bathroom

living room

dining room

kitchen

bedroom

bedroom

front yard

Get 2 points for every correct sentence/answer.

Round 1

In my kitchen, there's a garbage can below the window.

In my kitchen, there's a garbage can in front of the stove.

Round 2

In your house, where's the garbage can?

It's in the kitchen.

Is the garbage can next to the stove?

No, it isn't. It's in front of the stove.

Listen and check (✓) or write.

1 a  b

2 a 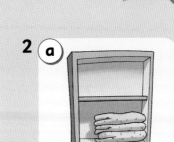 b

3 a  b

4 a  b

5 a 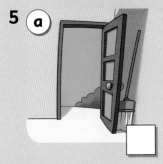 b

6 a  b

7 a  b

8 a  b

9 The _____ is _____ the stove.

10 Is the broom in the living room? _____

 I can describe my home.
I can find information/things with help from someone.

Now go to Space Island.

Review Units 3 and 4

1 B:24 **Listen and check (✓).**

2 **Ask and answer.**

Is the bird above the TV?

Yes, it is.

3 **Read and underline the four mistakes.**

This is my bedroom. It has a bed, a cupboard, a chair, a TV, and a lamp. There are two tables—a big table and a small table. The lamp is on the small table. It's next to the books. There are four books on the cupboard. I have a snake. It's in front of the cupboard. It's great!

 4 **Write T = True or F = False.**

1 There are plants behind the sink. ☐

2 There is a broom in front of the cupboards. ☐

3 There is a plant below the picture. ☐

4 The computer is on the sofa. ☐

1 (B:25) **Listen.**

ROSE   HARRY

2 (B:26) **Listen and say.**

a a baseball cap

b a belt

3 (B:27) **Listen and number.**

c a sweatshirt

d a sweatsuit

f a uniform

g a polo shirt

h shorts

i sandals

e **a blouse**

j **slippers**

4 B:28-29 **Listen and chant.** (See page 113.)

 B:30 **LOOK!**

What are you wearing?	I'm wearing	a baseball cap. shorts.
What's he/she wearing?	He's/She's wearing	
Are you wearing	a baseball cap? shorts?	Yes, I am.
		No, I'm not.
Is he/she wearing		Yes, he/she is.
		No, he/she isn't.

5 **Look at the scene. Write T = True or F = False. Then ask and answer.**

1		I'm wearing a sweatsuit.	☐
2		I'm wearing jeans and a sweatshirt.	☐
3		I'm wearing a skirt and a blouse.	☐

Look at Harry. What's he wearing?

Is he wearing shorts?

He's wearing sneakers.

No, he isn't.

 B:31 **Quest**

6 B:32 **Listen and say.**

a

scarf

b

beanie

c

ski jacket

d

wool sweater

e

tights

f

hiking boots

g

leather

h

fancy

i

plain

j

colorful

7 B:33-34 **Listen and circle. Then sing.**

SONG

Chorus:

Where's my red scarf? Where's my red scarf?

I have my (/   ),

my beanie, and my (/   ).

But not my red scarf! Not my red scarf!

My sister's in the bedroom. What's she wearing?

She's wearing my (/   ).

Is she wearing my scarf? No, she isn't. No, no, no!

(Chorus)

My brother's in the garden. What's he wearing?

He's wearing my (/   ).

Is he wearing my scarf? Yes, he is. Yes, yes, yes!

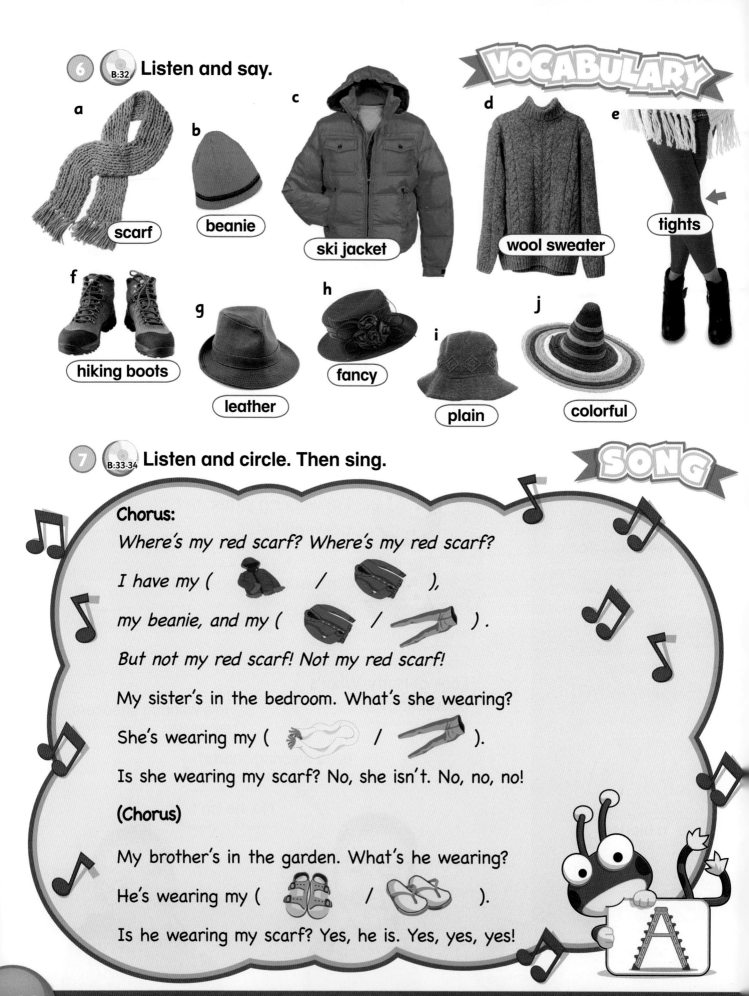

8 **Draw and color two favorite clothing items. Then say.**

5

B:35 **LOOK!**

This is	my favorite	scarf.
These are		tights.
I love my scarf/tights.		

Item 1

Item 2

This is my favorite scarf. It's red and blue.

9 B:36-37 **Read. Then listen and write.**

SKILLS

Costume party

Hi. I'm Hilda. I'm a pirate. I'm wearing a plain white shirt, and a black and red skirt. This is my favorite skirt. I'm wearing black leather shoes and white socks. Do you like my fancy hat?

I'm Ben. I'm a clown. My hair is orange. I'm wearing a big yellow T-shirt and big blue pants. These are my favorite shoes. And I love my colorful bow tie. Do you like it?

1 She's _____.

2 It's a _____.

3 He's _____.

4 It's a _____.

11 **Is Hop wearing red pants? Discuss your answers.**

64 Consolidation

12  **Match.**

1 Harry is wearing his favorite   hat.
2 Hop is wearing   orange.
3 Harry's pants are   a fancy T-shirt.
4 Hop is wearing his favorite   sneakers.
5 Harry is wearing   a new wool coat.

13 **Role-play the story.**

14 **Listen. Then write.**

 VALUES

 Be polite.

1 Please.

2 Excuse me.

3 Thank you.

4 You're welcome.

5 I'm sorry.

6 I'm happy for you.

a   When we get a gift, we say, "_____."

b   When we hurt someone, we say, "_____."

c   When we ask for something, we say, "_____."

d   When someone says, "Thank you," we say, "_____."

e   When someone tells us good news, we say, "_____."

f   When we want to get someone's attention, we say,

"_____."

HOME-SCHOOL LINK

Make a list of other polite English phrases. Show your family.

 PARENT

15 **Read. Then check (✓) the things you do.**

What can you do to help at home?

1 I can set the table. ☐

2 I can clean the bedroom. ☐

3 I can make the bed. ☐

4 I can wash the dishes. ☐

5 I can wash the car. ☐

 **THINK!**

What other things can you do to help at home?

 16 **Read and number the pictures.**

1 **Mom**: Amy, please set the table.
  Amy: OK, Mom.

2 **Mom**: Wow, your bedroom is clean! Good job, Amy!
  Amy: Thanks, Mom!

3 **Mom**: Amy, please make your bed.
  Amy: Sorry, Mom. I'm busy with homework.

4 **Mom**: Amy, clean your bedroom, please.
  Amy: I'm sorry, Mom.

5 **Mom**: Please, Amy. Wash the dishes.
  Amy: OK, Mom!

 **MINI-PROJECT** Make a poster of class chores.

SOUNDS FUN!

17 B:40 **Listen.**

1 **sc** 2 **sk** 3 **sm** 4 **sn**

5 **sp** 6 **squ** 7 **st** 8 **sw**

18 B:41 **Listen, point, and say.**

19 B:42 **Listen and blend the sounds.**

1 s – c – ar – f scarf
2 s – k – a – te skate
3 s – m – e – ll smell
4 s – n – i – p snip
5 s – p – oo – n spoon
6 s – qu – i – d squid
7 s – t – ar star
8 s – w – i – m swim

20 **Underline *sc*, *sk*, *sn*, *squ*, *st*, and *sw*. Read the sentences aloud.**

1 Look at the star!

2 Snip some hair.

3 See the squid swim.

4 Wear a scarf to skate.

(21) **Stick. Then ask, answer, and draw.**

 HAVE FUN!

 Stick

Are you wearing shorts?

Yes, I am.

No, I'm not. My turn.
Are you wearing a scarf?

 Guess!

Me

My friend

Now tell another friend:

This is my favorite ….

These are my favorite ….

I love my ….

 How to play

1 Students work in pairs.
Each student chooses
stickers of clothing items
for himself/herself.

2 Students play
rock-paper-scissors.
The winner is the first one
to try to guess the
clothing items his/her
friend has chosen.

If he/she guesses
correctly, he/she draws
the item in his/her friend
box. Students take turns
guessing.

3 Students keep asking and
answering until they have
guessed correctly and
finished their drawing.

(22) **B:43** **Listen and check (✓) or write.**

1 (a)  (b)  (c)

2 (a)  (b)  (c)

3 (a)  (b)  (c)

4 (a)  (b)  (c)

5 (a)  (b)  (c)

6 (a)  (b)  (c)

7 (a)  (b)

8 (a)  (b)

9 What's _____ wearing? _____ wearing a plain white _____ and a colorful _____.

10 _____ wearing a _____ ? _____, _____.

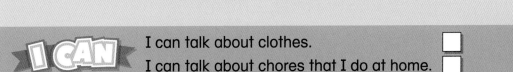
I CAN
I can talk about clothes. ☐
I can talk about chores that I do at home. ☐

TEACHER

 Now go to Space Island.

Wider world 3

School uniforms

1 🔘 B:44 **Listen and read.**

> My name's Clara and I'm from Mexico. In my school we don't have uniforms. Here, I'm wearing a plain red T-shirt, black pants, and my favorite sneakers. They're black and very comfortable.

> I'm Scott and I'm from the United Kingdom. My school is in Oxford and we have uniforms. I'm wearing a blue shirt, blue pants, and a blue jacket. I'm wearing my black leather school shoes.

2 **Write T = True and F = False.**

1 Clara is wearing a uniform. ☐

2 Clara is wearing her favorite sneakers. ☐

3 Scott is not wearing a uniform. ☐

4 Emma has a colorful pink bag. ☐

5 Jiaming is wearing a uniform. ☐

I'm Emma and I'm from Canada. I'm not wearing a uniform. I'm wearing a pink shirt and my favorite jeans. I love my pink bag!

My name's Jiaming. I'm from China. We have uniforms in my school. I'm wearing a white shirt, blue shorts, gray socks, and sandals. These are my favorite sandals.

 Ask and answer.

1 What are you wearing?
2 Are you wearing a uniform?
3 Do you like uniforms?

1 B:45 **Listen.**

2 B:46 **Listen and say.** **3** B:47 **Listen and number.**

a  run

b  ride a bike

c  catch a ball

e  play baseball

f  play tennis

g  play basketball

4 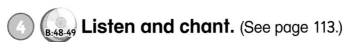 **B:48-49** **Listen and chant.** (See page 113.)

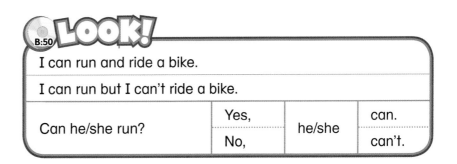

B:50 **LOOK!**

I can run and ride a bike.			
I can run but I can't ride a bike.			
Can he/she run?	Yes,	he/she	can.
	No,		can't.

5 **B:51** **Listen and match. Then ask and answer.**

1 Professor Bloom can …

2 Hip can …

3 Harry can't …

4 Harry can …

1. Can he run?

No, he can't.

d play soccer

h do taekwondo

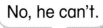 **B:52** Quest

6 B:53 **Listen and say.**

gym

baseball field

basketball court

running track

stadium

skating rink

ski slope

bowling alley

beach

swimming pool

7 B:54-55 **Listen and circle. Then sing.**

SONG

She was at the (soccer field / basketball court).

Can she play (basketball / soccer)?

Can she? Can she? Can she?

Yes, she can. Oh yes, she can.

She was at the (running track / baseball field).

Can she (play baseball / run fast)?

Can she? Can she? Can she?

Yes, she can. Oh yes, she can.

He was at the (gym / beach),

At the (gym / beach).

Can he (climb / jump) the rope?

Can he? Can he? Can he?

Yes, he can. Oh yes, he can.

LOOK! B:56

| I/He/She | was at the gym. |
| | wasn't at the gym. I/He/She was at the baseball field. |

8 B:57 **Listen and write ✓ = was or ✗ = wasn't. Then say.**

1

2

3

4

> She wasn't at the beach.
> She was at the stadium.

9 B:58 **Read. Then stick.**

 SKILLS

Monday, July 1st

I was at the Aquaworld Festival to watch the dolphin show. It was a lot of fun! Dolphins can't walk or run but they can swim 5 to 12 kilometers per hour and jump out of the water. They can jump through hoops and catch a ball. They have very strong fins. They are very clever animals. I love dolphins!

 Stick

1 Dolphins can …

a

b

c

2 Dolphins can't …

a

b

c

 What can Hoopla do? Discuss your answers.

12 **Number in order.**

a Hip, Hop, and Harry help Hoopla out of the water. ☐

b Hip, Hop, and Harry watch Hoopla climb a tree. ☐

c Hip, Hop, and Harry see Hoopla. ☐

d Hoopla catches a ball. ☐

e Hoopla falls into the water. ☐

f Hoopla dances. ☐

 13 **Role-play the story.**

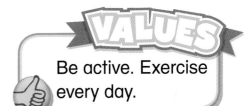

Be active. Exercise every day.

 14 **Write Y = Yes or N = No.
Then ask and answer.**

1

Me ☐ My friend ☐

Go walking.

2

Me ☐ My friend ☐

Go running or jogging.

3

Me ☐ My friend ☐

Go cycling.

4

Me ☐ My friend ☐

Do push-ups.

5

Me ☐ My friend ☐

Play sports.

6

Me ☐ My friend ☐

Practice martial arts.

Do you go walking?

Yes, I do.

HOME-SCHOOL LINK

Choose one activity to help keep you fit and active. Tell your family about it.

PARENT

15 B:60 **Listen and do.**

Stay fit! Stay healthy!

1 Stretch your arms up.

2 Bend your knees.

3 Twist your body to the left.

4 Twist your body to the right.

5 Turn around.

16 B:61 **Read. Then play.**

THINK!

What happens to our body when we don't exercise?

1 I say, Bend your knees.

2 I say, Turn around.

3 Jump.

4 You moved. You're out. Sit down, please.

Let's continue.

Useful words/phrases

Walk.   Jump.   Run.
Hop.   Shake your hands.
Clap your hands.

MINI-PROJECT

Make a list: Things I do to keep fit.

17 **B:62 Listen.**

1 bl　　**2 fl**　　**3 gl**　　**4 pl**　　**5 sl**

18 **B:63 Listen, point, and say.**

19 **B:64 Listen and blend the sounds.**

1 b - l - a - ck　black　　　**2** f - l - a - g　flag

3 f - l - oa - t　float　　　**4** g - l - a - ss　glass

5 p - l - u - m　plum　　　**6** p - l - a - te　plate

7 s - l - i - p　slip　　　　**8** s - l - ee - p　sleep

20 **Underline *bl*, *fl*, *gl*, *pl*, and *sl*. Read the sentences aloud.**

1 I want a glass of pink milk.

2 Go to sleep.

3 There's plum jam on the spoon.

4 Look at the black flag.

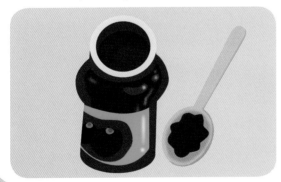

 **Play.**

He can run and jump.

She can play baseball but she can't play soccer.

✓ = can
✗ = can't

START

FINISH

FINISH

B

START

22 Listen and check (✓) or write.

B:65

1 (a)  (b)

2 (a)  (b)

3 (a)  (b)

4 (a)  (b)

5 (a)  (b)

6 (a)  (b)

7 (a)  (b)

8 (a) 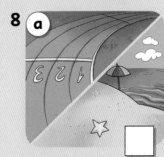 (b)

9 Can she _____? _____, _____.

10 Can he _____? _____, _____.

 I can talk about sports. ☐
I can talk about my abilities. ☐

TEACHER

Now go to Space Island.

Review & Assessment

Review Units 5 and 6

 Play.

① **Start**	② **Move** →	③ 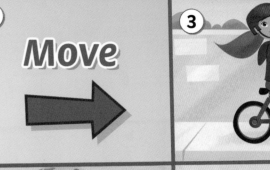
⑩ **Move** ←	⑨ 	⑧ **Miss a turn**
⑪ 	⑫ **Go to 9**	⑬ **Move** →
⑳ 	⑲ **Miss a turn**	⑱ 
㉑	㉒ **Go to Finish**	㉓ 

Miss a turn ④

⑤

⑦

Move ⑥

⑭

⑮

Go to 23 ⑰

⑯

Miss a turn ㉔

Finish ㉕

How to play

Can you ride a bike?

Is he wearing a sweatshirt?

7 Food

1 C:02 **Listen.**

2 C:03 **Listen and say.**   **3** C:04 **Listen and number.**

a

peas

b

mangoes

c

carrots

d

cucumbers

f

oranges

g

peaches

h

potatoes

i

tomatoes

4 C:05-06 **Listen and chant.** (See page 113.)

C:07 **LOOK!**

Do you	like	peas?	Yes, I do.
			No, I don't.
Does he/she			Yes, he/she does.
			No, he/she doesn't.

5 C:02 **Listen. Then read and circle.**

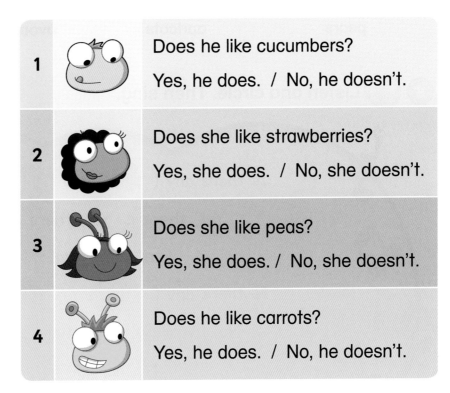

1		Does he like cucumbers? Yes, he does. / No, he doesn't.
2		Does she like strawberries? Yes, she does. / No, she doesn't.
3		Does she like peas? Yes, she does. / No, she doesn't.
4		Does he like carrots? Yes, he does. / No, he doesn't.

6 **Look at Activity 5. Ask and answer.**

1. Does he like cucumbers?

Yes, he does.

e plums

j strawberries

C:08
Quest

7 C:09 **Listen and say.**

a

broccoli

b

lettuce

c

spinach

d

cabbage

e

pears

f

apricots

g

avocadoes

h

cherries

8 C:10-11 **Listen and circle. Then sing.**

SONG

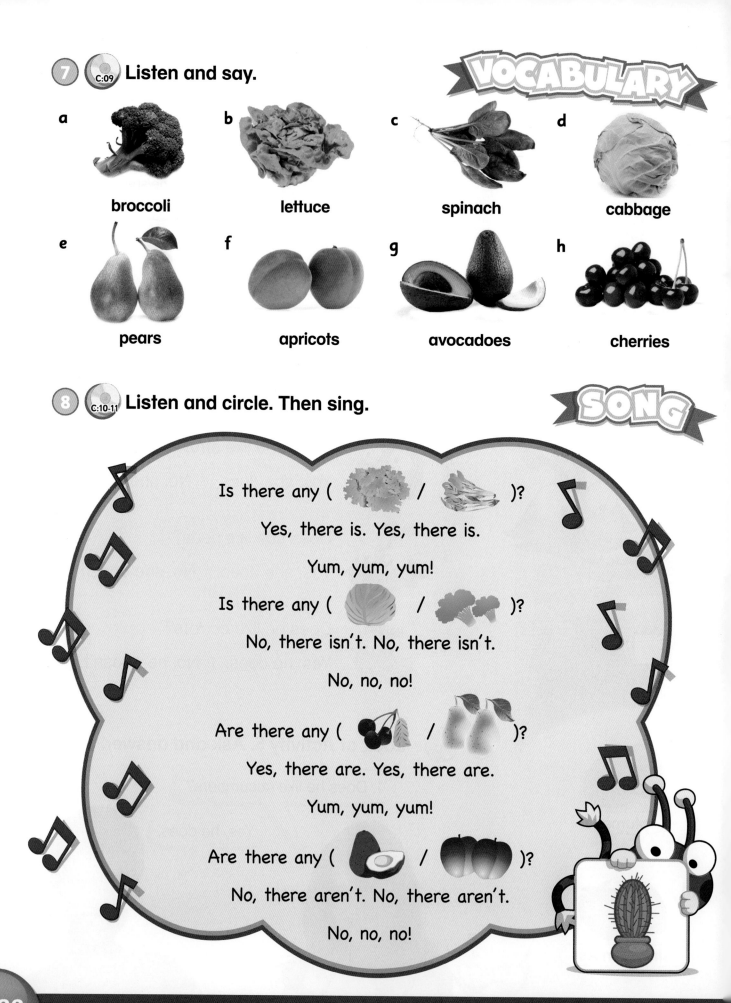

Is there any (/)?

Yes, there is. Yes, there is.

Yum, yum, yum!

Is there any (/)?

No, there isn't. No, there isn't.

No, no, no!

Are there any (/)?

Yes, there are. Yes, there are.

Yum, yum, yum!

Are there any (/)?

No, there aren't. No, there aren't.

No, no, no!

C:12 LOOK!

Is there any broccoli?	Yes, there is.
	No, there isn't.
Are there any pears?	Yes, there are.
	No, there aren't.

9 **Stick five foods.
Then ask and answer.**

Are there any carrots?

Yes, there are.

 Stick

10 **C:13-14 Read. Then listen and write.**  SKILLS

Lisa Martin Astronaut

Reporter: Hello, Lisa. Do you have breakfast in space?
Lisa: Yes, I do. Breakfast, lunch, and dinner.
Reporter: Is there any fruit?
Lisa: Yes, there is. I eat strawberries for breakfast. Yum! I also eat yogurt.
Reporter: Do you like pears and avocadoes?
Lisa: I like avocadoes, but I don't like pears.
Reporter: Are there any vegetables for lunch or dinner?
Lisa: Yes, there are. I like to eat tomatoes but I don't like spinach.
Reporter: Thank you, Lisa.

1 _____   2 _____

3 _____   4 _____

12 **What food colors can Hip and Hop eat? Discuss your answers.**

88 Consolidation

13  **Check (✓).**

1 Hop likes …

2 Rose and Hip like …

3 Hip doesn't like …

14 **Role-play the story.**

15 **Write Y = Yes or N = No.
Then ask and answer.**

VALUES

Stay healthy. Eat more fruit and vegetables.

🌙		Me	My friend
1 corn ☺		☐	☐
2 eggplant ☺		☐	☐
3 pizza 😐		☐	☐
4 orange juice ☺		☐	☐
5 fries 😐		☐	☐
6 burger 😐		☐	☐
7 bananas ☺		☐	☐
8 soda 😐		☐	☐

Do you like to eat corn?

Yes, I do.

HOME-SCHOOL LINK

Make a list of healthy foods. Tell your family.

16 C:16 **Read. Then check (✓) the unhealthy food.**

GRAINS	FRUIT AND VEGETABLES	PROTEIN	DAIRY	FATS AND SUGARS

Do you like healthy food? Look at the food groups. Pasta and bread are in the orange group. Cakes and candy are in the red group. The red group isn't very healthy. In the blue group there are cheese and yogurt. There are eggs, meat, and fish in the purple group. In the green group, there are fruit and vegetables. They are very healthy. Do you like fruit and vegetables?

- [ ] **Fats and sugars**   cakes, candy, chocolate
- [ ] **Dairy**   milk, cheese
- [ ] **Protein**   eggs, meat, fish, chicken
- [ ] **Fruit and vegetables**   plums, strawberries, peaches, potatoes, beans, peas, tomatoes, cucumbers, carrots
- [ ] **Grains**   bread, pasta

THINK!
Is the tomato a fruit or a vegetable?

17 **Say the word. Find the food group.**

Potatoes. Green group!

MINI-**PROJECT**   Make a class food survey.

18 (C:17) **Listen.**

| 1 **br** | 2 **cr** | 3 **dr** | 4 **fr** |
| 5 **gr** | 6 **pr** | 7 **str** | 8 **tr** |

19 (C:18) **Listen, point, and say.**

20 (C:19) **Listen and blend the sounds.**

1 b – r – ow – n   brown   2 c – r – a – b   crab

3 d – r – o – p   drop   4 f – r – o – g   frog

5 g – r – ee – n   green   6 p – r – e – ss   press

7 s – t – r – i – ng   string   8 t – r – ai – n   train

21 Underline *br*, *cr*, *fr*, *gr*, *pr*, *str*, and *tr*. Read the sentences aloud.

1 Press to go up.

2 Look at the green frog.

3 The crab is brown.

4 Pull the train with the string.

22 Play.

Does he/she like …?

Is/Are there any …?

HAVE FUN!

How to play

1 Students work in pairs. They play rock-paper-scissors. The winner is the first one to roll the dice and spin the paper clip on the board. He/She must say the question and answer according to the space the paper clip points to.

2 Students take turns rolling the dice and spinning the paper clip. A student gets 1 point for every correct question and 1 point for every correct answer.

3 Students must mark the spaces they land on. A studer cannot land on a space that was previously taken eithe by him/her or the other student. When all the spaces a taken, students will add up their points. The student w more points wins.

23 C:20 **Listen and check (✓) or write.**

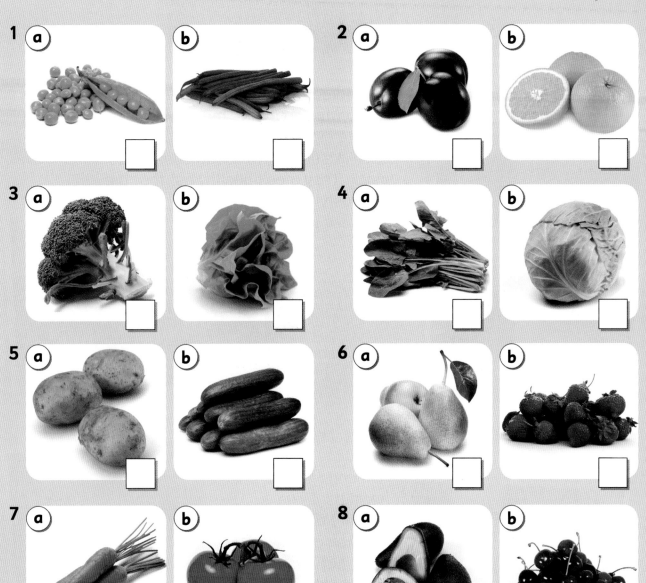

1 **a** **b**

2 **a** **b**

3 **a** **b**

4 **a** **b**

5 **a** **b**

6 **a** **b**

7 **a** **b**

8 **a** **b**

9 Is there any _____? _____

10 Does he like _____? _____

 **I CAN**
I can talk about food. ☐
I can talk about likes and dislikes. ☐

 TEACHER

 Now go to Space Island.

1 **Listen and read.**

I'm Andrea. I'm from Argentina. I don't like potatoes but I like meat. My favorite dinner is *asado* or barbecue. I also like chocolate sandwiches for a snack. They aren't healthy but they are very tasty!

asado

My name's Zeki and I'm from Turkey. Here I have fantastic pastries with pistachios, almonds, and walnuts. I love them. I also like chicken and fruit, but I don't like kebabs.

pastries

2 **Match.**

1 Zeki	chicken and fruit
2 Berta	fruit and vegetables
3 Andrea	pizza and pasta
4 Kay	chocolate sandwiches

3

My name's Kay. I'm from Jamaica. My favorite lunch is jerk chicken with rice and peas. It's a traditional dish. Yum! I also like meat patties. I love them and they're very healthy. I also like fruit and vegetables, but I don't like pumpkin soup.

meat patties

jerk chicken

4

I'm Berta and I'm from Italy. My favorite dinner is pizza with cheese and tomatoes. I also like pasta and ice cream. Chocolate ice cream is delicious, but I don't like strawberry ice cream.

3 **Ask and answer.**

1 Does Andrea like *asado*?
2 Does Zeki like pastries?
3 Does Kay like pumpkin soup?
4 Does Berta like strawberry ice cream?
5 What's your favorite food?

1 C:22 **Listen.**

a sleeping

b reading

c eating

d drinking

f walking

g dancing

h doing homework

i listening to music

4 C:25-26 **Listen and chant.** (See page 113.)

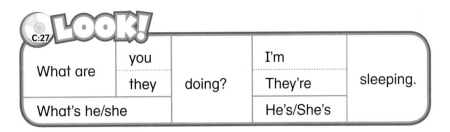

C:27 **LOOK!**

What are	you	doing?	I'm	sleeping.
	they		They're	
What's he/she			He's/She's	

5 **Look at the scene. Write T = True or F = False.**

1		He's reading.	☐
2		She's doing homework.	☐
3		She's eating and drinking.	☐
4		He's sleeping.	☐

6 **Act, ask, and answer.**

What are you doing?

I'm reading.

e **cleaning**

j **making a machine**

C:28 **Quest**

Presentation / Practice

Asking and answering about actions **97**

7 C:29 **Listen and say.**

a singing

b playing the piano

c playing the violin

d playing the trumpet

e playing the flute

f quietly

g loudly

h quickly

i slowly

j terribly

8 C:30-31 **Listen and stick. Then sing.**

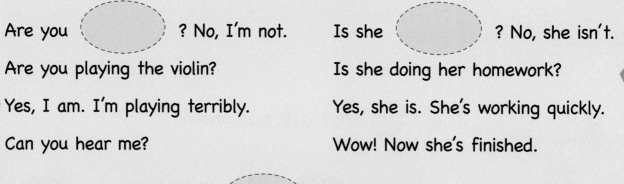

Are you ⬭? No, I'm not.

Are you singing? Yes, I am. I'm singing quietly. Can you hear me?

Are you ⬭? No, I'm not.

Are you playing the violin?

Yes, I am. I'm playing terribly.

Can you hear me?

Is she ⬭? No, she isn't.

Is she doing her homework?

Yes, she is. She's working quickly.

Wow! Now she's finished.

Is she ⬭? No, she isn't.

Is she dancing? Yes, she is. She's dancing slowly.

Wait! Now she's finished.

Stick

Are you singing?	Yes, I am. / No, I'm not.
Is he/she singing?	Yes, he/she is. / No, he/she isn't.
Is he/she singing quietly?	Yes, he/she is. / No, he/she isn't. He's/She's singing loudly.

9 **Choose and write. Then play charades.**

What are you doing? I'm _____.

Is he playing the piano loudly?

Yes, he is.

10 **Read. Then write.**

SKILLS

Dear Grandma and Grandpa,
We're at the beach. It's sunny and hot. I'm drinking water and reading a book quietly. Tim is sleeping and Dad is playing the violin. He's playing very loudly! ☹ Mom isn't here. She's walking slowly on the beach. I can see her now. She's waving hello! We're all having fun! Please come next time.

Tracy

1 What is Tracy doing? She's _____ and reading.

2 Is Tim playing volleyball? No, _____. He's _____.

3 What is Dad doing? He's _____.

4 Is Mom running on the beach? No, _____. She's _____
_____.

Listen and read.

12 Who helps Professor Bloom to fix the machine? How?
Discuss your answers.

13 **Match.**

1 The machine is   Earth.

2 Professor Bloom is telling Hoopla   to come to Earth one day.

3 They are going back to   goodbye.

4 Hip and Hop are saying   working now.

5 Harry is telling Hip and Hop   to run quickly.

 14 **Role-play the story.**

 15 **Write Y = Yes or N = No.**
Then ask and answer.

VALUES

Learn new things.
Develop your talents.

1 Me ☐ My friend ☐
Sing.

2 Me ☐ My friend ☐
Dance.

3 Me ☐ My friend ☐
Act.

4 Me ☐ My friend ☐
Paint.

5 Me ☐ My friend ☐
Cook.

6 Me ☐ My friend ☐
Play an instrument.

Can you sing? Yes, I can.

HOME-SCHOOL LINK
Make a list of new skills you would like
to learn. Show your family.

Flying machines

This is a rocket. It's very big, but it can fly. Rockets can fly in space very quickly. There are three astronauts in this rocket.

This is a hot-air balloon. It's flying on hot air. It doesn't have wings, but it can fly. There is a pilot. He's flying the balloon. He's flying very carefully.

1   Does the hot-air balloon have wings? _____

2   Is the pilot in the hot-air balloon flying carefully? _____

3   Can rockets fly in space? _____

4   Do rockets fly very slowly? _____

THINK!

Can you name two more flying machines?

MINI-PROJECT

Use paper to make and decorate your own flying machine.

17 C:36 **Listen.**

| 1 **ft** | 2 **mp** | 3 **nd** |

| 4 **nt** | 5 **sk** | 6 **sp** | 7 **st** |

18 C:37 **Listen, point, and say.**

19 C:38 **Listen and blend the sounds.**

1 l – e – f – t left

2 b – u – m – p bump

3 h – a – n – d hand

4 w – i – n – d wind

5 p – ai – n – t paint

6 a – s – k ask

7 w – i – s – p wisp

8 n – e – s – t nest

20 **Underline *ft*, *mp*, *nd*, *nt*, *sk*, and *st*. Read the sentences aloud.**

1 I have a bump on my leg.

2 The bird is in the nest.

3 This is my left hand.

4 Ask the artist to paint a cat.

21 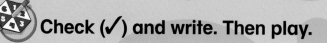 **Check (✓) and write. Then play.**

quickly
slowly
quietly
loudly
terribly

Are you playing the piano?

No, I'm not.

Are you playing the violin?

Yes, I am.

Are you playing the violin quietly?

Yes, I am.

Round 1				
Me				
My friend				
Round 2				
Me				
My friend				
Round 3				
Me				
My friend				

How to play

1 Students work in pairs. Each student chooses an instrument and writes how he/she plays it (e.g., quickly).

2 Students play three rounds. They play rock-paper-scissors at the start of each round to determine who will start first. The winner is the first one to ask a series of questions until he/she guesses his/her partner's choices or until his/her time runs out. (Note: Each student has limited time to make a guess.) If he/she guesses correctly, he/she must check and write his/her guess in the correct space.

3 The student with more correct guesses at the end of the third round wins.

Listen and check (✓) or write.

1 ⓐ  ⓑ

2 ⓐ  ⓑ

3 ⓐ  ⓑ

4 ⓐ  ⓑ

5 ⓐ  ⓑ

6 ⓐ  ⓑ

7 ⓐ  ⓑ

8 ⓐ  ⓑ

9 What's _____? _____

10 Is _____ playing _____? _____

 I can talk about things that my friends and I are doing.
I can talk about my talents.

 TEACHER

Now go to Space Island.

Review 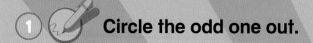 Units 7 and 8

1 Circle the odd one out.

fish
meat
eggs
chicken
chocolate
pasta

cleaning
reading
sleeping
drinking
eating
doing homework

2 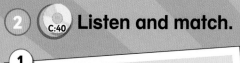 Listen and match.

1

2

3

TRACY

TIM

Act, ask, and answer.

1

2

3

4

5

6

What are you doing, Tim?

I'm sleeping.

Goodbye

C:41 **Listen, find, and point.**

2 C:42 **Listen and number.**

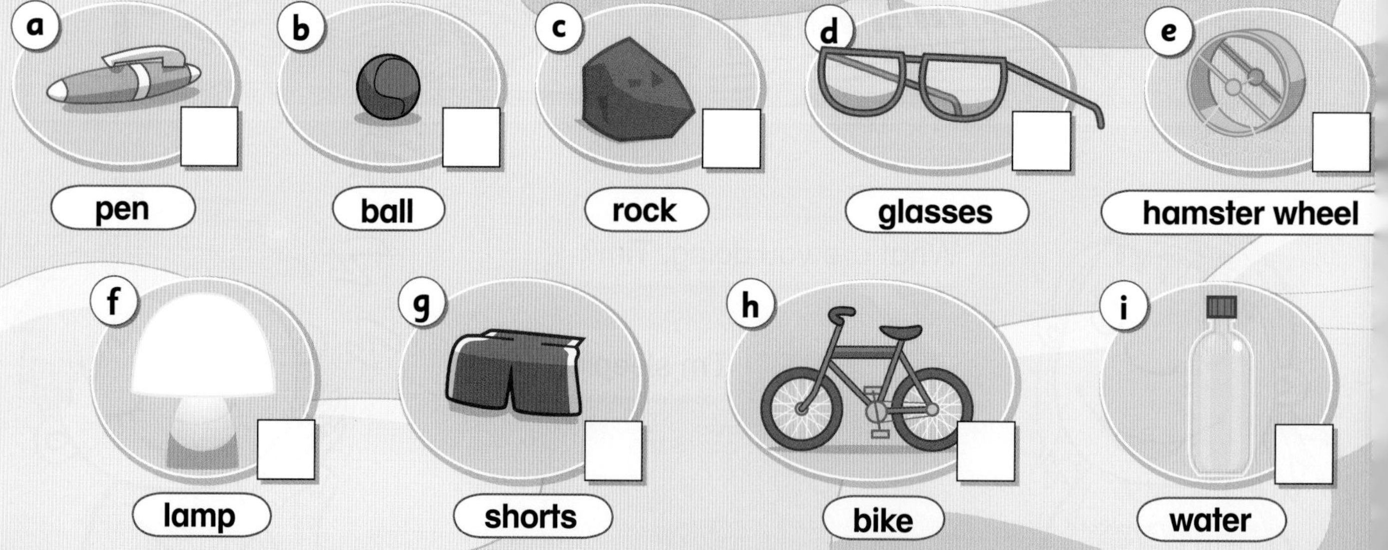

a
pen

b
ball

c
rock

d
glasses

e
hamster wheel

f
lamp

g
shorts

h
bike

i
water

3 C:43-44 **Listen and write. Then sing.**

Look up, down, here, there.

Look around everywhere.

We have the pen, the ball, the _____, the glasses,

the hamster wheel, the _____, the shorts, the bike, and

the _____! We have them all. It was _____!

Come on, come on, come on a quest today!

Now Harry, Rose and the Professor are flying home to Earth.

Say goodbye to Hip and Hop. Say goodbye one more time.

Goodbye, _____. Goodbye, _____.

See you again another day!

4 **Ask and answer.**

My favorite character is ….

My favorite story is about ….

My favorite song is about ….

1 Who's your favorite character?
2 What's your favorite chant about?
3 What's your favorite song about?
4 What's your favorite story about?

5 **Draw or stick pictures. Then write.**

My favorite nature scene

There is _____ .

There are _____

_____ .

There aren't any _____ .

My pet

My pet is a _____ .

It has _____ .

It doesn't have _____ .

It is so _____ .

I love my pet _____ .

6 **Draw or stick a picture of you in your home. Then write.**

This is me in my _____

_____ (room).

I have _____ hair

and _____ eyes.

I'm wearing _____

and _____ . These are

my favorite clothes.

My _____ (room) is great

There is _____ .

There are _____ .

7 🖊 **Draw or stick pictures of what you can or can't do. Then write.**

I can _____

_____.

I can _____

_____.

I can't _____

_____.

8 🖊 **Draw or stick pictures of your family. Then write.**

My _____ likes

_____.

_____ doesn't like

_____.

My _____ is

_____

_____.

Unit 1 Nature

4 | A:18 ············· page 13

There's a pond, a blue pond.
There's a rock, a brown rock.
There's an animal, a purple animal.
Look at the sun!
Look at the clouds!

There are birds, blue birds.
There are insects, pink insects.
There are flowers, yellow flowers.
Look at the sun!
Look at the trees!

A:19 ·············· Karaoke version

Unit 2 Me

4 | A:37 ············· page 25

I have black hair.
I have brown eyes.
I don't have glasses!

Look, it's Dad!

She has brown hair.
She has big, brown eyes.
She doesn't have glasses!

Look, it's Grandma!

A:38 ·············· Karaoke version

Unit 3 Pets

4 | A:57 ············· page 37

What does it look like?
It has two eyes.
Does it have four legs?
No, it doesn't.

What does it look like?
It has a tail.
Does it have two paws?
No, it doesn't.

Splish, splash, splish
It's a fish!

A:58 ·············· Karaoke version

Unit 4 Home

4 | B:05 ············· page 49

There's a mirror in the kitchen.
Yes, there is. That's right!

There's a picture above the sink.
Oops! There isn't. No, no, no.

There's a plant behind the bed.
Yes, there is. That's right!

There's a mirror above the sofa.
Oops! There isn't. No, no, no.

B:06 ·············· Karaoke version

Unit 5 **Clothes**

 .... page 61

Hey, hey! What are you wearing?
I'm wearing sandals.
Hey, hey! What are you wearing?
I'm wearing a sweatsuit.

Hey, hey! What are you wearing?
I'm wearing a baseball cap.
A cap?
That isn't a cap. They're shorts!

B:29 .... Karaoke version

Unit 6 **Sports**

B:48 .... page 73

I can't climb!
But I can jump!
Jump, jump, jump!
I can jump so high!

She can run
But she can't dance!
Run, run, run!
She can run so fast!

He can play soccer
And ride a bike.
Ride, ride, ride!
He can ride so well!

B:49 .... Karaoke version

Unit 7 **Food**

 .... page 85

He likes peas.
He doesn't like plums.
Oh no, no.
He doesn't like plums.

She likes strawberries.
She doesn't like beans.
Oh no, no.
She doesn't like beans.

C:06 .... Karaoke version

Unit 8 **Things we do**

 .... page 97

What are you doing?
I'm drinking, I'm drinking.

What are you doing?
I'm cleaning, I'm cleaning.

What are you doing?
I'm sleeping, I'm sleeping.

C:26 .... Karaoke version

Word list

Acknowledgments

The Publishers would like to thank the following teachers for their suggestions and comments on this course:

Asako Abe
JiEun Ahn
Nubia Isabel Albarracín
José Antonio Aranda Fuentes
Juritza Ardila
María del Carmen Ávila Tapia
Ernestina Baena
Marisela Bautista
Carmen Bautista
Norma Verónica Blanco
Suzette Bradford
Rose Brisbane
María Ernestina Bueno Rodríguez
María del Rosario Camargo Gómez
Maira Cantillo
Betsabé Cárdenas
María Cristina Castañeda
Carol Chen
Carrie Chen
Alice Chio
Tina Cho
Vicky Chung
Marcela Correa
Rosalinda Ponce de Leon
Betty Deng
Rhiannon Doherty
Esther Domínguez
Elizabeth Domínguez
Ren Dongmei
Gerardo Fernández
Catherine Gillis
Lois Gu
SoRa Han
Michelle He
María del Carmen Hernández
Suh Heui
Ryan Hillstead
JoJo Hong
Cindy Huang
Mie Inoue
Chiami Inoue
SoYun Jeong
Verónica Jiménez
Qi Jing
Sunshui Jing
Maiko Kainuma
YoungJin Kang

Chisato Kariya
Yoko Kato
Eriko Kawada
Sanae Kawamoto
Sarah Ker
Sheely Ker
Hyomin Kim
Lee Knight
Akiyo Kumazawa
JinJu Lee
Eunchae Lee
Jin-Yi Lee
Sharlene Liao
Yu Ya Link
Marcela Marluchi
Hilda Martínez Rosal
Alejandro Mateos Chávez
Cristina Medina Gómez
Bertha Elsi Méndez
Luz del Carmen Mercado
Ana Morales
Ana Estela Morales
Zita Morales Cruz
Shinano Murata
Junko Nishikawa
Sawako Ogawa
Ikuko Okada
Hiroko Okuno
Tomomi Owaki
Sayil Palacio Trejo
Rosa Lilia Paniagua
MiSook Park
SeonJeong Park
JoonYong Park
María Eugenia Pastrana
Silvia Santana Paulino
Dulce María Pineda
Rosalinda Ponce de León
Liliana Porras
María Elena Portugal
Yazmín Reyes
Diana Rivas Aguilar
Rosa Rivera Espinoza
Nayelli Guadalupe Rivera Martínez
Araceli Rivero Martínez
David Robin
Angélica Rodríguez

Leticia Santacruz Rodríguez
Silvia Santana Paulino
Kate Sato
Cassie Savoie
Mark Savoie
Yuki Scott
Yoshiko Shimoto
Jeehye Shin
MiYoung Song
Lisa Styles
Laura Sutton
Mayumi Tabuchi
Takako Takagi
Miriam Talonia
Yoshiko Tanaka
María Isabel Tenorio
Chioko Terui
José Francisco Trenado
Yasuko Tsujimoto
Elmer Usaguen
Hiroko Usami
Michael Valentine
José Javier Vargas
Nubia Margot Vargas
Guadalupe Vázquez
Norma Velázquez Gutiérrez
Ruth Marina Venegas
María Martha Villegas Rodríguez
Heidi Wang
Tomiko Watanabe
Jamie Wells
Susan Wu
Junko Yamaguchi
Dai Yang
Judy Yao
Yo Yo
Sally Yu
Mary Zhou
Rose Zhuang